TWIN TONGUES

TWI N T ONG U ES

Claire Lacey

SNARE

Invisible Publishing
Halifax & Toronto

Library and Archives Canada Cataloguing in Publication

Lacey, Claire, 1987-, author
    Twin tongues / Claire Lacey.

(Robert Kroetsch Award for Innovative Poetry)
Poems.
ISBN 978-1-926743-42-4 (pbk.)

    I. Title.

PS8623.A338T85 2013   C811'.6   C2013-905675-0

Edited by Jon Paul Fiorentino

Design by Megan Fildes | Typeset in Laurentian and Slate
With thanks to type designer Rod McDonald

Printed and bound in Canada

Invisible Publishing | Halifax & Toronto
www.invisiblepublishing.com

We acknowledge the support of the Canada Council for the Arts which last year invested $20.1 million in writing and publishing throughout Canada.

Invisible Publishing recognizes the support of the Province of Nova Scotia through the Department of Communities, Culture & Heritage. We are pleased to work in partnership with the Culture Division to develop and promote our cultural resources for all Nova Scotians.

Canada Council   Conseil des Arts
for the Arts   du Canada

To the users. To the anxiety.

WRITING THROUGH INDE

WHAT has Independence done to me as a Papua New Guinean, a writer, and scholar of indigenous cultures? Surely, this question must be asked by many conscientious Papua New Guineans.

Papua New Guinea as a postcolonial nation struggles to free itself from a colonised history, more particularly from the neocolonial practices and influences of its former coloniser. Achieving political Independence has never freed Papua New Guinea completely from Australia.

Australian influence in Papua New Guinea is deeper than perceived at the political level. Australia continues to play a major part in the economic, social, and political development of Papua New Guinea. The relationship between Australia and Papua New Guinea is often tested, but always maintained through diplomatic dialogues and other political processes.

Early Papua New Guinea writings tackled Australian colonialism with fervent and nationalist fury to the extent of achieving Independence without bloodshed. The literature of that period is fuelled by such political necessity.

After Independence Papua New Guinean writers disappeared, except for a few committed ones, who continue to write. Two notable figures of the period are Russell Soaba and Paulias Matane, who continue to write literary and non literary works beyond the 2000s.

Soaba continues to write and publish PNG.

Paulias Matane continued moved away from the Aimb led him to publish many ne even after becoming the th Guinea. Grand Chief Sir Pa New Guineans to publish the us.

These gentlemen are, to m bodiment of a legacy that reflu to speak about their condit Reading their works helps us

The writings of the 1980s presence, dependent relations reassessment of the changing Guinea. Papua New Guinea issues of identity, social chan the movement between village ing up, adolescence, education conflicting cultural situations.

PNG, 37 YEARS ON

INDEPENDENCE celebrations in Papua New Guinea remains colourful and vibrant year after year.

Merging the various culture into that particular special day is indeed a testament of how diversified this island nation is. Throughout the country, everyone had their own way of

they were of their identity, culture and most important their 37-year-old nation.

Young and old flocked to the Independence Hill on the slight showering morning of 16 September. The slight drizzle could not contain the glitter that shone from the eyes of those witnessing the moment when the

make his official address, flag took its first feel of its space.

And indeed it was spectacular sight.

Children hoisted on fathers' shoulders and one w managed to bring along puppy stood tall watching flag fly high.

Ten flags installed by t National Capital Distri Commission at the 5-Mile Jac

WAKA BALLO

MES APA GUMUNO

HTY Jiwaka regional ballot boxes kept in a container were burnt to ashes during the early hours of la g.

Electoral Commission was in the process of m er to Kiminiga police barracks in Western Highlan l Court order was taken out by losing regional cand member for Anglimp-South Waghi Jamie Maxton 13.

property manager of Waghi Klos building, w ers for the three open electorates and regional bal ept, said some men armed with high powered guns t a security guards looking after the containers an s of the container on fire around 3.10am

manager, John Minji, told The National that the men threatened the security guards, who ran for co the Waghi Klos.

y then broke the lock to the main gate and went g, he added.

independence on Sept 16, 1975.
The visit by Prince Charles signifies the standing PNG has with the British crown.

Group leader Alderton was tight-lipped about details of the royal visit but assured Papua New Guineans that Prince Charles and his wife were looking forward to meeting many people.

"We won't be going into details of the visit but we will go back and talk to the royal highnesses about our visit here," Alderton said.

"It's very much a people's jubilee so the royal couple would like to connect with many people."

Alderton said apart from the visit to Port Moresby, the royal highnesse couple would be travelling outside the capital city but he did not specify where they would

oup was met by chief ial protection).
and Supt Tim Nash manager), Joshua Puls Andy Tibble (tour Harrison (press secretary designate), imon Martin (deputy assistant private designate to the royal the royal couple), Joy n and commonwealth ction (Private secretary ice party private yesterday afternoon arrived in Port man from Buckingham vance party of six men

 stralian Prime Minister trd and that the royal couple sit for five days from er spending two days in

"Touch me
with the tongue of your
lan lan lang
language
l/anguish
  anguish
English
is a foreign anguish"

M. NourbeSe Philip, "Discourse on the Logic of Language"

A Short History of English

d   v   n   c

The beginning of everything

Bipo bipo tru God i mekim kamap skai na graun na olgeta samting i stap long en. Tasol graun i no bin i stap olsem yumi save lukim nau. Nogat. Em i stap nating na i narakain tru. Tudak i karamapim bikpela wara na spirit bilong God i go i kam antap long en. Na God i tok olsem, "Lait i mas kamap." Orait lait i kamap. God i lukim lait i gutpela, na em i amamas. Na em i brukim tudak na tulait. Tulait em i kolim "De," na tudak em i kolim "Nait." Nait i go pinis na moning i kamap. Em i de namba wan.

Bihain God i tok olsem, "Na ol pisin i mas kamap na flai nabaut long skai." Orait God i mekim kamap ol kain kain pisin. Kotkot i lap nogut tru. Em i de namba faiv.

Hello Jasper.

Tok Pisin

Tok bilong mami. Tok bilong mi. Babu no save long Tok Pisin. Mi no save gut long Inglis. Husat i save long tok Inglis? Husat i save long tok Inglis? Pisin. Inglis.
Do you recognize your daughter, English? Mi no harim tok bilong yu.

Bipo ~~tok boi. tok waitmen, tok masta~~. Tok gel? Em nau! Nem bilong mi em Tok Pisin Inap yu senisim tok bilong mi? Husat i save long tok Tok Pisin? Miksim English na Tok Pisin.

Maski long planti toktok! Mi pilim sik!

For immediate translation:

I am writing poetry in a language

within which I am ignorant. Sorry.

English keeps a crow.

Jasper sits on a sandpaper perch.
Watches pigeons through gnawed bars,
through window's glass. Pigeons
purr in the sunshine. Jasper turns first
his right eye, then his left to watch
the sun-speckled pigeons stroll along the balcony.

English puts a record on when she
leaves the house: Parakeet Training Record.
"Hello," says the firm lady voice. "Hello baby."
Jasper would rather hello baby the radio
were on, hello so he could whistle with hello
baby the golden oldies ten till noon, commercial hello-free.

The pigeons crash the hello baby sky. Orange tabby
kerthumps into the space. Jasper squawks,
flaps dusty wings. A scatter of loose feathers
and fluff. Orange tabby hops onto the balcony rail,
out of the door's frame, out of sight.

Jasper lifts up left foot,
beaks a claw. Hello baby. Hello.

New Guinea Pidgin is a strange universal language a scream-
ingly funny way of speaking a comical sing ingenious
terrible arbitrarily pruned language a ous mishmash
a hotchpotch ugly jargon the most t language to
learn in the world a dreadful parody Anglo-Saxon
language ghastly mutilated English a t caricature of
English a peculiar crossbred physiogn credibly prim-
itive with amazing simplicity of cannib e primitiveness
the most dreadful language of all.

Saveman bilong ol tok ples mekim pasi gut.

Tok Pisin is a language is a dialect is a va v of English is a
New English is a pidgin is a creole is a s d language is a
first language is a mother tongue is an c al language is a
regional dialect is a lingua franca is a ne language is an
english is not English is a hundred years is a spectrum is
a group is a family is a colonial language plantation lan-
guage is a colonized language is a slave uage is a racial-
ized language is a radical language is a li ted language is
a standardized language is a nonstandard riety is a literary
language is an educational language is an ban language is
an uneducated language is not instituti lized is used in
government debate is not used in gover ent documents
is on the rise is in decline is spoken m than written is
studied and analyzed by foreign speaker English.

Watch my mouth splits standard language

From the hallway I can hear Jasper humming along with the radio, though he stops as soon as I turn into the doorway carrying a bucket and a bundle of newspaper. Hello Jasper! How are you today? Jasper, can you say hello? Hello! Hello Jasper. I open yesterday's newspaper, shifting the pages to cover the whole table. Jasper turns his head to watch me with his right eye. He sidles left on his perch as I approach. I open the cage and Jasper hops into the opening then onto the table. What do I have for you today? I pull a Ziploc baggy out of my pocket. It squishes in my hand: stewing beef cut into small cubes. I open the baggy and put it down for Jasper who reaches in and pulls a cube out in his beak. That will keep him busy. I open the cabinet next to the cage and pull out a black garbage bag, unfold it, and flick it open hanging it from the back of a chair. First I remove his perches and his rope toy, since those must be air dried. I dunk them into the soapy water in the bucket, then use a sponge to scrub them clean before laying them out on a paper towel on the floor. The tray at the bottom of the cage slide it out the newspaper mucked with two days worth of

the tray, dry it with paper towel, and then put it aside. The cage disassembles into three sections. Each section must be thoroughly washed and dried. His food and water dishes are easiest to clean, wide and shallow with no tricky places for dirt to catch. I line the tray with four layers of old news. I replace the pieces of the cage, except the perches and the rope. I go back into the cabinet and take out his alternate perches. One is a real branch with hooks attached at either end so that it can be set on the bars of his cage. This rope toy dangles a mirror, so that Jasper won't get lonely when I'm not in the room.

Jasper has eaten most of the beef. Red juice drips from his beak onto the weather forecast. He has one cube hidden in his throat pouch and another two in his beak to cache in his cage. He hops inside, looking for a good hiding place. Once again he doesn't find one, so he opens his mouth and lets the beef fall to the bottom. Splat. Splat. Splat. He looks in the mirror and wipes the juice off his beak onto the wood of his perch.

Pigeon

Columba livia is common pigeon, carrier pigeon, homing pigeon, rock pigeon,
rock dove

is urban vermin a member of the family Columbidae spoiled by classification a pest a rat with wings a disease carrier mi pilim sik domestic funny looking feral flies with a swimming motion in the air overpopulated easily hunted an inexpensive food source an ugly bird bluish health hazard historically important present nuisance.

travels in flocks must be discouraged inhabits public spaces produces acidic excrement should not be fed will not explode if fed rice though I used to frighten my sisters with that story can be frightened with imitation owls or falcons or strings of CDs hung across the balcony.

can be trained to transport, to deliver, to return.

cannot be taught to talk.

Dear Friends,

As you may know, I am currently working with the school board in Port Moresby in Papua New Guinea to share my experience with the local English teachers. Some are teaching English as a Second Language and some are teaching English as a subject. Like our own education system, Papua New Guinea's classrooms are desperately underfunded. Additionally, the literacy rate here is below 50%. Parents who cannot read usually do not have books for their children to learn from, which makes it all the more essential that each classroom has some books.

I am in a position where I can distribute materials directly to teachers and schools. I have already given away all the picture books I brought with me. If you have gently used picture books, chapter books, young adult novels, workbooks, etc., please consider donating them to children who need age-appropriate reading material to help them learn to read. Literacy can give these children a better future.

With appreciation,

English

the infringement of a tongue on another tongue

english wasn't invented

she flew out of mulching mouths

Mi no wokim wanpela samting i rong.

English wants to take the bus—the Public Motor Vehicle rather—on her first day of teaching English to primary students at a public school. She joins the crowd at the street corner. English notices that she is the only white person. She tells herself there's nothing to be nervous about. The first PMV arrives and English thinks that's smaller than I expected a city bus to be. English can't make out the shouted destination, it was maybe going to the market, the words come too fast, the press of bodies towards the shabby vehicle, the number seven painted white on the side, she steps aside to let other passengers through and the PMV drives away before she can ask the conductor if this is the bus she needs. A second PMV comes screaming up and clatters away. Number 9.

It would be more prudent to walk, English decides. She doesn't want to be late for her first day. Long strides down the street clutching the strap of her bag. English turns red.

Despite early teething problems the power's out. He doesn't understand you. Watch out for shortages or tomorrow. Don't say that. Soup's on the lack of this ingredient. Mind the gap. I can reach the low notes if I touch my chin to my neck, which means I have the biggest range of attributed speech incidents. Pick a peck of parrots. These manners uncalled for when cannibals. Voiceless bilabial plosive muddled alveolar nasal voiceless alveolar sibilant. Je voodoo salute Mary. It's archaic in its newest edition predicated by years of careful research into the precise dialect spoken in the leeward shade of the mountain. I am the them that occupies. Distribute directly the materials. Vowels are emotion. We found that out on Easter Sunday of all days. A short intake of breath followed by a long inhale. Numbers and emergencies around town. Submerge. Apply the syntax immediately to reduce swelling.

tok: a message, an account, a word, a speech; **salim tok i go long ples** send a message home; 2 to tell, to say, to speak; **no ken tok olsem** don't say that.

pisin 1 a bird; **ol pisin i save plai long skai. 2** a clan, a totem; **yu bilong wanem pisin?** to **what clan do you belong?**

If you want him to speak you must split his tongue. If you want him to speak you must split his tongue. If you want him to speak you must split his tongue. If you want him to speak you must split his tongue. If you want him to speak you must split his tongue. If you want him to speak you must split his tongue. If you want him to speak you must split his tongue. If you want him to speak you must split his tongue. If you want him to speak you must split his tongue. If you want him to speak you must split his tongue. If you want him to speak you must split his tongue. If you want him to speak you must split his tongue. If you want him to speak you must split his tongue. If you want him to speak you must split his tongue. If you want him to speak you must split his tongue. If you want him to speak you must split his tongue. If you want him to speak you must split his tongue. If you want him to speak you must split his tongue. If you want him to speak you must split

Bidialectical

mishmash system of shit and piss
on concrete, acidic. Cannibalistic birds
stripped of class collect on statues
in squares.

Mutilated Inglis emerges boiled
beak of crow.
Grandma's caw
arbitrarily pruned.

Train your ugly daughter to reject
urban jargon, but her corvis tongue slips
into hotchpotch dialect despite your best effort
to inflict stricture.
Neutral tongues sicken dreadfully.
Daughter speaks pigeon to mother,
crow to grandmother;

coos to boys, clacks at girls.

Talk pigeon. Talk crow.

Locals appreciate travellers trying their language no matter how muddled you may think you sound. Try dispella mixmasta belongum jesus kryst.

Fledgling crow has a beak too big for his face. First flight a series of falls from branch to branch. He hasn't grown into altitude. Mama caws from her perch. Fledgling hops into a bush and stays very very still.

Clumsy human hands reach into the bush and scoop fledgling crow up. Mama cries in her tree, but doesn't condescend. She has other mouths to mulch.

In 1953 the United Nations suggested that Tok Pisin, a co-lonial language, should no longer be used in Papua New Guinea. In 1953 the United Nations recommended that Tok Pisin, a pidgin language with roots in English and German, should no longer be used in Papua New Guinea. In 1953 the United Nations suggested that Tok Pisin, a language adopted by slaves and labourers, should be abandoned by the people of Papua New Guinea. In 1953 the United Nations recommended that Tok Pisin, the most common lingua franca in Papua New Guinea, should no longer be used. In 1953 the United Nations suggested that Tok Pisin, one language on an island with over 200 languages, should no longer be used. In 1953 the United Nations recommended that Tok Pisin should no longer be used in Papua New Guinea, a country administered by the government of Australia. In 1953 the United Nations suggested that Tok Pisin should no longer be used in Papua New Guinea.

miningi bilong dispela stori

save long tok tru.

PIDGIN

Hello Jasper! Can you say hello Jasper? Hello. Hello. Hello. Can you say hello? H. El. Lo. Just give it a try. Hello Jasper. Hello.

must to if split speak want his you him if split

Grandmother Tongue

Language standardization has systematically worked against the underclass as well as women.

Systems of guilt and language built on the strength of my Grandmother's tongue.
Gauge the weight of linguistic guilt systems. Strictness of language burdens my tongue with systems of guilt, my Grandmother's strength, her words, my worth. Grandma, for standards of strength in language we are guilty.

In Grandmother's system, signals of class are standard. Split standard language stigma. Sick of the weight of tongues I stand on the system. Grandma or strands of language splitting. If standards, strength. If splits, guilt. Spitting at standards to alleviate guilt. Stand for or against the language stricture of the word class,
the tongue class, the language classification of standards.

I am guilty of tongues and words.

Worth of words, Grandma, or guilty strands. Is your guilt my guilt, of systems of stands? Gauge the system of standardized words. Work against my split tongue, sick language. A non-standard system of tongues devalues the weight of my worth. Words emerge from language and tongues: system of wanting or worth. To stand and spit on systems of standards takes strength. Withdraw from snarled systems, strict structure of tongue, of Grandmother language. Split the stricture or standards stick. To stand on the strength of my Grandmother's tongue is to standardize the weight of my guilt.

Sick of the weight of class, I language.

Non-gaging of standards the system sickness. Speak in one tongue, or many, to distinguish self from system. Tonguing against guilt. Other tongues are struck, split, spoilt by classification. Strike the system with other standards. Ease the stigmas of tongues and self. Declassify the state of language, the strength of words (signal others of approaching guilt) secretly language mystifies standards with splits. Multiply tongue with other to slip outside the standards. Disengage from burdened language to gain diverse tongues. With words, a stand.

English is surprised that this rain is a monsoon. She imagined a downpour out of disaster relief news clips. This is just heavy rain, really. English puts her dress shoes and socks and a towel in a bag and rolls up the legs of her pants. Yesterday her feet didn't dry out all day, she got home and they were peeling and wrinkled. It's windy enough that she doesn't bother with her umbrella, though she puts that in her bag too, in case the wind abates. Her neighbourhood is at the top of a small hill, the street is a sluiceway she has to follow down to the PMV stop. English hoped the rain would clear the air. She's never felt humidity like this before, sticky humidity that dampens English when she steps outside, her deodorant washed away by sweat. Everything stinks in the heat. Thank god there's air conditioning at the house, when the power works anyways. But the rain doesn't do much for the smell, or the heat. Emma told her the wet won't last long, that the monsoon season here isn't comparable to other parts of the country. The rainy season in Port Moresby is short and hard, she said. Typically it's pretty dry here. But the rain isn't hard enough yet, English figures. She shudders at the squelch of her sandals in the brown water. She jumps whenever debris brushes against her ankles—mostly leaves and sticks but who knows what else is down there. "I've got to get some rain boots," English mutters. She images taking off her chaffing sandals and splashing barefoot through the water. The pavement would be cool and rough enough to ease her itching soles. She could use her toes to pick up pebbles and plonk them back into the stream, or kick up water like the laughing children whose spatters are ignored by the already drenched passersby.

I cannot sever a twin tongue—strangling one to strength-
en the stricture of strictness standards slacken, slip out-
side structure words, sense of worth, or less, submerge in
a shifting system, find a tongue or an other tongue stand
by your tongue, outside the strands of guilt is language.
my womb of words is mothering tongues, infant systems.
Grandma, meet your daughter language: built from your
word cyst stem, outside your language class, let her gage
words free of guilt within a whole tongue or many. words
become her streng.

By ALISON ANIS

COUNTING for the national
population and housing census
has faced hiccups since Monday,
most notably the shortage of
census pads for data entry,
according to an official. Some
officers yesterday claimed they
were still to be paid their K40
daily allowances.

Kila Geberi, the census
coordinator for the Southeast
region which included Central,
Northern, Milne Bay and NCD,
said most census teams around
the c... ...ry had stoppe... ...work...
b... ...e was

interv...
"The ...shortfall of
pads thr... . the count.
we also ...ore... intervi...
guides ...al," Gebe...
"We may have underes...
the workload and distan...
earlier assessments of w...
formation."

Geberi said: "The nu...
people in the househ...
grown over the 10-ye...
and, because there a...
small villages scatter...
...mote areas, most of...
...icers are now f...
...slem) durin...
"He sai...

English tells the room full of teachers that for the duration of this workshop they should pretend to be primary students learning a second language. English demonstrates imperative sentences: stand up. Jump. Touch your nose. Open the door. Close the door. Pick up a pencil. Draw your favourite place. English then provides the theoretical framework of her lesson. Teachers must contextualize linguistic input and foster language awareness for better student learning outcomes. For a month she monitors teaching acts so that she can offer teachers and teacher trainees feedback on lessons. English lends herself as a model speaker. Hello, my name is English. How do you do? She participates in several classrooms as an assistant. Then she is off to the next school to work with a new group of teachers and students, where she repeats her contextualized linguistic input in an attempt to foster language awareness. It is essential, English knows, to provide contextualized linguistic input in order to foster language awareness. It is impossible to foster language awareness without contextualized linguistic input. That's just common sense.

Mama screams by the window. English moves the cage away. Scat, you're scaring him! Jasper beats his wings, croaks I'm here. Don't go. English beats on the glass and the crow startles into the sky.

S Y N D
S T L A
E M N G
O F U A
G U G E
I L G U
T A N S

The power is out. Again. English smacks her desk, the long email to her mum lost with the electricity. This wouldn't happen back home. At least it's sunny today, during the wet season the clouds make the blackout really depressing. English had planned to make lunch after finishing her email, but now she doesn't want to open the fridge and let the cold out just in case the outage lasts more than a couple of hours. English signs. Stretching her arms above her head, she gets up from the chair and feels the pop in her lower back. Upstairs, Jasper is shouting at the radio, upset that it turned off in the middle of a song. Emma's not home, or English could win back some paper clips at cards. English thinks about work, this would be a good time to review Freire, but ornery she picks up the first Harry Potter book instead and goes to sit on the front step. Mr. and Mrs. Dursley, of number four, Privet Drive, were proud to say that they were perfectly normal, thank you very much. They were the last people you'd expect to be involved in anything strange or mysterious, because they just didn't hold with such nonsense.

Pidgin English Anglophone Edition

this is how you say piano: bikpela bokis biling krai taim yu paitum na kikim en or old man in my house; you hit him white teeth, he laugh; you hit him black teeth, he cry. That particular posh television voice says that the word for a helicopter is dispella mixmasta belongum jesus kryst quite interesting.

the word for piano is piano.

A small boy was using what I'd have called a machete and what the locals call a bush knife or a busnaip to cut a bunch of bananas off a tree. The knife was longer than his arm. Emma, my Australian housemate, gave me a bush knife as a welcoming gift—everyone here carries one she said laughing. Don't worry. They're mostly used for gardening. I was dubious, wondering what kind of garden would require a small sword, but it's true. I've seen them used to trim branches from bushes and to edge lawns. My knife is safe under my bed. Not once have I seen a hacking, though I've read about them in the newspaper.

Last year's fledgling took a turn guarding the nest when Mama and Papa crow both went to feed. He hopped from one side of the nest to the other eyes intent on the nestlings. He bobbed his head, opening his empty beak above cheeping gullets until parents brought home a bit of hare or chicken or pizza or baggie. A bulge stuck in one nestling's throat. She could not cheep for food, her unfeathered wings stopped flapping. One morning she was pushed from the nest by the other nestlings as they shoved to be first fed.

A pigeon pair nests in the tree in front of the balcony window. Jasper echoes their domestic chatter. He's got their accent down now. The pigeons take no notice.

Jasper has never been in the snow. He has never hidden food in powder that turns into a crust overnight so that it takes persistent pecking to get to the cache. He has never slid down a snow-covered roof then flapped up to do it again.

The Effect of Learning Environments
on Second Language Acquisition

Institutional environments where language
in the case of a child or student
immerse target in the learner
system explains what the error is

Watch My Mouth

th thhh thhhh the
interdental articulation
place tongue between
teeth tight restriction
airflow mechanics

Authentic fluency is taught
to learners content-based
or communicative native
speaker accent correction
identity negotiation in progress
to be graded on written and oral

Repeat After Me

I go punting down the Cam.
You go punting down the Cam.
He goes punting down the Cam.
She goes punting down the Cam.
We go punting down the Cam.

the
this
that
they
their
then
three
those
thou
though
through
throw
thrive
thrift
thin
thine
thrush
thrash
thrust
throat
threat

I go

LECT

They go punting down the Cam.

Learner errors are divided into types
the influence of L1 on L2 the impediment
of a tongue on another tongue

Try It Yourself

How these difficulties are
overcome the personal pedagogy
of the tongue (inductive)
in a second language setting
fossilization a natural environment
is preferred

Crate learner and drop in midst of L2 speakers
native speakers of the standard
variety will have a positive influence
(deductive) of foreigner talk
rather than teacher talk
though it may be condescending
it is ideal
for the ego
once traces
of L1 have faded
replaced by new language id

te
tis
tat
tey
teir
ten
tree
tose
tou
tough
trough
trow
trive
trift
tin
tine
trush
trash
trust
troat
treat

Is she a baby? Language standardization just didn't hold with such nonsense. Narapela tang. I cough phlegm feathers into my hand. Damp yellow chords. Peculiar crossbred physiognomy supposed to be their constitutional duty. Ugly crow perches on crocodile beak. The ethical ouch of speaking. A glottal glop. Make mine a double-double. Can I sit next to you girl. God I hate it here. How to talk in betel nut red and lime green. Bai ren i pundaun. I'll buy one. You say tomato and I say inedible. Subject, as implied. The ecology doesn't require such distinction. It's just speech done dirt cheap.

Blood spills out of his beak and for a moment I think he's just got some raw beef in his mouth. But he doesn't, and I know that because I'm the one that cut him. I didn't think there would be so much he's too small for all this blood. When I was eight I fell out of bed and split the upper labial frenulum and my mother came running before I knew I was crying. We can't do anything for a cut in your mouth, she said. But I wanted a Band-Aid to stop the gush. Try not to swallow, and she gave me a bowl. I didn't think of that until now what was I thinking was I thinking I wasn't. He's keeping very very still and maybe I could cauterize it. If I heat the knife and hold it against the cut? But his beak seems smaller and my fingers aren't steady I've killed him I've killed him no stop panicking he's alive my fingertips know the thrumming impulse rattles his body. I wanted Jasper to talk to talk back to me so I opened his beak and. Why did I trust that book why didn't I ask a vet but I was stupid so stupid. Let him be okay I don't even just let him be okay he'll be okay so small and cut I cut him. I saved him from the ground I wrapped him in cloths he was warm and fed and safe he was safe. I wrap a blanket around Jasper and I sing hush-a-bye don't you cry go to sleep my little birdie. I lose my voice before the bleeding stops.

New Guinea Pigeon

New Guinea Pigeon is a strange universal bird a screamingly funny way of speaking a comical amusing ingenious terrible arbitrarily pruned bird a wondrous mishmash a hotchpotch ugly jargon the most difficult bird to learn in the world a dreadful parody of the Anglo-Saxon bird ghastly mutilated Crow a very apt caricature of Crow a peculiar crossbred physiognomy incredibly primitive with amazing simplicity of cannibalistic primitiveness the most dreadful bird of all.

Yumi go na lukluk long ol pisin.

Pisin i bird i dialect i variety of Crow i New Crow i pigeon i creole i second bird i first bird i mother hen i official bird i regional dialect i lingua franca i neutral bird i crow i not Crow i hundred years old i spectrum i group i family i colonial bird i plantation bird i colonized bird i slave bird i racialized bird i radical bird i liberated bird i standardized bird i nonstandard variety i literary bird i educational bird i urban bird i not an educated bird i not institutionalized i used in government debate i not used i government documents i rise i decline i spoken more than written i studied and analyzed by foreign speakers of Crow.

S Y D L
S T A N
E M G U
O F A G
G U E S
I L O U
D E N D

I buy jars of baby food. The first day, Jasper doesn't eat though I put Beef & Carrot mush into his feeding bowl. The second day he takes a bit of Turkey & Gravy. The third day he eats half the jar of Sweet Potato and a few spoonfuls of Beef & Gravy. I rinse his mouth with salt water from a syringe and he tries to scratch me. Good bird, Jasper. You'll feel better soon.

I had measles when I was little and I couldn't go out for Halloween. I couldn't even give candy at the door because I was contagious. I sat in the window in my witch costume, with my spotty face painted green watching all the other kids trick-or-treat. I know how you feel.

brick language bullet wall

ها
says th
tually reve
and people liv

lich
to help

"We found out
some ghost names
and that the descrip
houses were made
said.

ner ministry
at building
the city to
ish and Tok

He said this was evi
places lik ... P

ll be on the
ecause we

English reaches the end of a row of vendors, out of the way of merchandise displayed on blankets on the ground and tables along the street. Radios burst reggae music and static. The woman selling dresses laughs at something her customer says. The hand drawn signs are mostly in Tok Pisin, as is the chatter that pulses along the market street. The sellers yell "Wait mari! Wait mari!" as she passes, but Inglis isn't shopping today. Inglis pulls a tube of sunscreen out of her new purple and blue bilum purse. After refreshing her sunscreen and adjusting her floppy tourist hat, she wanders away from the market. She looks at the houses flaking colourful paint. Laundry hangs from second floor windows. A woman trims a hedge with her buisnap, long sweeps of the knife fluttering green leaves into the air. On the other side of the road a red parrot squawks from the branches of a palm tree. Inglis walks another block, two. She turns a corner and stops. To her right a burnt out brick house is missing a roof. In front of her, a man is aiming a gun at the wall. His head jerks up and his eyes widen. The wall is covered in dozens of little holes. Inglis stares. There is no smoke in the air, but the smell of strong cigarettes lingers. The gun moves slowly, the man points it at the ground, though he still holds it in both hands ready. He says something. His voice sweats. One dusty black boot steps towards her. Cigarette butts squished on the ground behind the boots. English doesn't recognize the language. Louder he repeats himself. The syllables won't resolve themselves into familiarity. The gun isn't as shiny as the ones on tv. It's bigger, a machine gun, something out of a gangster movie. Sweat dampens her bra. He gestures with his chin, pushing it forwards.

His face is clean-shaven, he's maybe twenty. She puts her hands up in front of her body and steps back. A mosquito buzzes around English's head, landing near her ear. Its feet tickle her skin and her cheek twitches. The man wears green pants, green jacket with top button undone. English says I'm leaving, I'm sorry, and walks backwards. The heel of her sandal catches on the cracked asphalt. She jars her ankle and wavers but doesn't fall. She backs around the corner before she lets her hands drop to her sides. English opens her mouth and breathes. She feels her ribs opening with her lungs, her heart, blood pumping into her head. Her feet return her to the market, past the market, turn her up the hill towards the gates of home.

Jasper chews his nails. English walks by his cage and turns off the radio.

Jasper slowly lowers his foot to his perch.
"Fuck you," he says.

Systems of crow and tongue built on the strength of my Grandmother's tongue.

Gauge the weight of linguistic crow systems. Strictness of tongue burdens my tongue with systems of crow, my Grandmother's strength, her words, my beak. Grandma, for standards of strength in tongue we are crowing.

In Grandmother's system, signals of class are standard. Split standard tongue stigma.

Sick of the weight of tongues I stand on the system. Grandma or strands of tongue splitting. If standards, strength. If splits, crow. Spitting at standards to alleviate crow. Stand for or against the tongue stricture of the word class,   the tongue class,   the tongue classification of standards.

I am crowing of tongues and words.

Beak of words, Grandma, o_ _ _ _ing strands. Is your crow my crow, of systems of sta_ _ _ _ _ _ system of stan-dardized words. Work ag_ _ _ _ _ _ _ _ le. A non-standard system_ _ _ _ _ my beak. Words eme_ _ _ _ tem of wanting or b_ _ _ standards takes str_ _ _ _ _ _ _ _ _ns, strict structure o_ _ _ _ _ _ _lit the stricture or _ _ _ _ _ _ _ _ _ n of my Grandmo_ _ _ _ _ _ _ t of my crow.

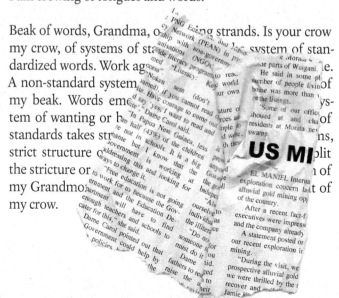

piano

(ceci n'est pas un piano)

Yu bilong

English is a cat is a cache 22.

wanem pisin?

Jasper has never barrel-rolled. His wings are full but there's no room. He opens his wings and turns a circle on his perch. His feathers brush bars.

Kotkot i lap nogut tru. When the little crow created God, she laughed for the rest of the week.

B I N P
P O L E
T O N T
K P I T
I S O K
I N P L
B I E S

Inglis has learned the motion of the PMV. Most have hinged doors that remain open, though some are missing their doors entirely. The conductors rapidly yell the destination as they approach the bus stop. Inglis still can't always make out the truncated words, but she has memorized the routes by number. If there aren't many people waiting sometimes the vehicle doesn't quite stop. There is a trick of grabbing the doorframe and using it to swing aboard. On weekends the PMVs are irregular, but during the week they are mostly reliable. White people generally don't use the PMV, but Inglis was warned that as a woman alone she shouldn't take a taxi. Besides, Emma's been using the PMVs for over a year without incident. The number nine is an old PMV, Inglis thinks it's probably been chugging along since the early seventies, but it has recently been painted white with bright blue trim. English squeezes in the door and hands the conductor one kina, moving to an empty seat three rows in. The conductor passes the two coins that make up her thirty toea change to the man in the first row, who hands it to the woman behind him who gives it to Inglis. It's thirty-two degrees and humid, and the PMV seems slower than usual, its engine whining in the heat. On a steep hill, the engine gives up and goes quiet, the van starts rolling backwards until the driver applies the break. The conductor tells the passengers to get out: it's time to push. The passengers groan. Inglis disembarks with the others, and walks along the side of the road as four of the passengers and the conductor get behind the bus and strain to get it up the hill. The other three passengers shout their encouragement, and Inglis joins in as the PMV approaches the top. When the driver tries to get the engine going again, it stalls. The conductor gives the side of the van a little kick. On the next try, the engine putters and coughs and the van begins to move. The conductor pats the PMV and gets back in, helping the passengers into the moving vehicle. Inglis makes it to work twenty minutes late and dusty from the road, but with a smile. She is pleased to finally have a story of her own to add to the staff-room complaints about the fickle condition of the PMVs. Inglis feels like she's fitting in.

Inglis says, "I'm glad you're here to listen Jasper." Inglis says, "I love you Jasper. Mi laikim yu tru. You're a good bird, yes you are."

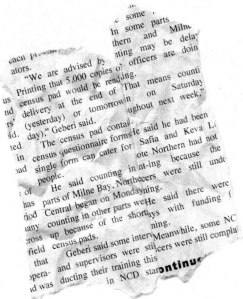

In some parts thern and Milne ating may be dela officers are doin

"We are advised by Printing that 5,000 copies o census pad would be reading. delivery at the end of That means counti (yesterday) or tomorrow in on Saturday day)," Geberi said. ughout next week."

The census pad contai in census questionnaire forms le said he had been single form can cater for Safia and Keva L people. ote Northern had not

He said counting in nt-ing because the parts of Milne Bay, Northecers were still und Central began on Monday ning.

counting in other parts we He said there were cross up because of the short ays with funding f field census pads.

Geberi said some interv Meanwhile, some NC and supervisors were sti cers were still compla ducting their training this in NCD star**ontinu**

Stepping into language infected by phonetics. Strut on the wrong side of the railing. I pull a black feather from my throat, the gag-tickle of flight. Hacking mutual unintelligibility. I imitate Dick Van Dyke's Irish vocal coach's interpretation of a Cockney accent. It's ah jolly oliday wiv Mary! Is there a punch line? Occasionally I throw in a Barney for authenticity. Apt caricature belongum jesus kryst. Humidity slinks west. It said 'ave Maria. Cover your mouth when you cough. It's polite. So the next feather caught in a napkin, how fancy. Pip pip let's go punting before tea, old bean.

a peculiar crossbred tongue so deeply etched

Advice to White Tourists: in the colonial past, Pidgin English was used to 'talk down' to the locals and many Papua New Guineans prefer to be addressed in English rather than in bad Tok Pisin by visitors. Tok Pisin bilong mi i go mobeta nau?

as women tongue tongue for guilt
stigma language guilt class standards
words stands a from of of of guilt
language to split of of tongue gain stand

Jasper tears strips from the newspaper at the bottom of his cage. He grasps the corner of a page and pulls, the satisfying growl of ripping paper. The shreds piled behind him, a mess of words and shit. Inglis opens the door to the room, Jasper, what are you doing over there? Jasper ignores her. Jasper, you're making a mess. That's enough of that. Jasper pumps his wings, the paper flurries out behind him, escaping the bars. Some fronds attach themselves to English, her face, her blouse, the white and grey paste that is said to be lucky when coming from above, but is just bird shit from below.

English leaves the room in a slurry of words. Jasper turns to watch her go. "Speak English!" he crows as she closes the door.

E   G   E   T

A   S   Y

G   N   S

A   L   H   T

T   E   G

I   H   N   A

S   S   C

Language has systematically worked.

Two little girls climb the guava tree in front of the house. The first time I came out to say hello they scarpered, the taller one scolding the shorter in rapid Tok Pisin for dropping the fruit they had picked.

I left the fruit in a pile beside the tree.

Now the taller one waits at the bottom while the shorter passes down the guavas. The girls ignore me.

My neighbour, a sun-pinked doctor from the UK tells me not to encourage them. They'll be into my pineapples next. I really should have a word with the gatekeeper. If he's letting these kids in, who knows who else is getting by?

"Oh they're just children," I say. I don't say it's not like I'm going to climb the tree. He'd rather leave the fruit to the birds.

Advice to Inglis turis: *Crocodile*

Fuck you! I'm a crow! Fuck you! I'm a crow! Fuck you! I'm a
crow! Fuck you! I'm a crow! Fuck you! I'm a crow! Fuck you!
I'm a crow! Fuck you! I'm a crow! Fuck you! I'm a crow! Fuck
you! I'm a crow! Fuck you! I'm a crow! Fuck you! I'm a crow!

Fuck you! I'm a crow! Fuck you! I'm a crow! Fuck you! I'm a
I'm a crow! I'm a crow! I'm a fucking crow! I'm a crow! I'm a
crow! Fuck you! I'm a crow! Fuck you! I'm a crow! Fuck you!
crow! I'm a fucking crow! I'm a crow! I'm a crow! I'm a fuck-
I'm a crow! Fuck you! I'm a crow! Fuck you! I'm a crow! Fuck
ing crow! I'm a crow! I'm a crow! I'm a fucking crow! I'm a
you! I'm a crow! Fuck you! I'm a crow! Fuck you! I'm a crow!
crow! I'm a crow! I'm a fucking crow! I'm a crow! I'm a crow!
Fuck you! I'm a crow! Fuck you! I'm a crow! Fuck you! I'm a
I'm a fucking crow! I'm a crow! I'm a crow! I'm a fucking
crow! Fuck you! I'm a crow! Fuck you! I'm a crow! Fuck you!
crow! I'm a crow! I'm a crow! I'm a fucking crow! I'm a crow!
I'm a crow! Fuck you! I'm a crow! Fuck you! I'm a crow! Fuck
I'm a crow! I'm a fucking crow! I'm a crow! I'm a crow! I'm
you! I'm a crow! Fuck you! I'm a crow! Fuck you! I'm a crow!
a fucking crow! I'm a crow! I'm a crow! I'm a fucking crow!
Fuck you! I'm a crow! Fuck you! I'm a crow! Fuck you! I'm a
I'm a crow! I'm a crow! I'm a fucking crow! I'm a crow! I'm a
crow! Fuck you! I'm a crow! Fuck you! I'm a crow! Fuck you!
crow! I'm a fucking crow! I'm a crow! I'm a crow! I'm a fuck-
ing crow! I'm a crow! I'm a crow! I'm a fucking crow! I'm a
crow! I'm a crow! I'm a fucking crow! I'm a crow! I'm a crow!
Fuck you! I'm a crow! Fuck you! I'm a crow! Fuck you! I'm a
I'm a fucking crow! I'm a crow! I'm a crow! I'm a fucking
crow! Fuck you! I'm a crow! Fuck you! I'm a crow! Fuck you!
a fucking crow! I'm a crow! I'm a crow! I'm a fucking crow!
I'm a crow! I'm a crow! I'm a fucking crow! I'm a crow! I'm
you! I'm a crow! Fuck you! I'm a crow! Fuck you! I'm a crow!

The crows tell the pigeons, and the cat, and the cars, and the telephone wires. They tell magpies and squirrels and stop signs and streetlamps. They tell puddles and trees and sunlight and clouds. Jasper hears the murder outside. Their caws collect inside the room, rattle the bars of his cage. He calls out but the words slip through the hole in his tongue. In his dreams, the crows speak English.

Legend

Clippings taken from *The National*, an English language PNG newspaper.

The Bible in Tok Pisin by the Bible Society of Papua New Guinea

Eri, Vincent. *The Crocodile*. Jacaranda Press, 1970. Print.

An explanation of pidgin myths can be found in *Oh, What a Blow That Phantom Gave Me!* at mediatedcultures.net/phantom/pmng.html

Kumaravadivelu, B. *Beyond Methods: Macrostrategies for Language Teaching*. New Haven: Yale University Press, 2003. Print.

A list compiled by Hoeltker from the German literature on Tok Pisin, quoted in *Tok Pisin Texts: From the beginning to the present* eds. Peter Mühlhäusler, Thomas E. Dutton, Suzanne Romaine. 1.

Parakrama, Arjuna. *De-Hegemonizing Language Standards: Learning from (Post)Colonial Englishes about 'English'*. New York: St. Martin's Press, Inc., 1995. Print.

SNARE

THE SNARE IMPRINT is home to exceptional, experimental poetry and prose. It represents part of Invisible Publishing's ongoing committment to a culture and tradition of literary innovation in Canada.

If you'd like to know more, please get in touch. **info@invisiblepublishing.com**

Invisible Publishing
Halifax & Toronto